ETHNIC IDENTITY,

The Case of
The French Americans

James Hill Parker

Long Island University
The Brooklyn Center

WITHDRAWN

UNIVERSITY
PRESS OF
AMERICA

LANHAM • NEW YORK • LONDON

Copyright © 1983 by

University Press of America,™ Inc.

4720 Boston Way
Lanham, MD 20706

3 Henrietta Street
London WC2E 8LU England

Library of Congress Cataloging in Publication Data

Parker, James Hill.
    Ethnic identity, the case of the French Americans.

    Bibliography: p.
    1. French–Canadians–United States–Ethnic
identity. 2. Ethnicity–United States. I. Title.
E184.F85P37   1983   305.8'114'073   82–23718
ISBN 0–8191–2981–X
ISBN 0–8191–2982–8 (pbk.)

To my wife Alice

and my children James and Lisa

RELATED WORKS BY THE AUTHOR:

Parts of the research of this book were reported
in the following publications:

James Parker, "The Assimilation of French
Americans," in Human Organization, Vol. 38,
Number 3, Fall 1979.

        and

"The French of New England Are Getting Nearly
Speechless," New York Times, Nov. 25, 1979,
p. 18E.

A discussion of my major findings on
French American assimilation.

Table of Contents

Preface

Preface

I became interested in the French-Americans as a
child, growing up in the midst of French people in
Auburn, Maine. Faced with a different culture, I soon
found it necessary to cope with it, and proceeded to
form impressions based upon my experience. Not only
did I have first-hand experience with the French culture, but also my parents, relatives, and "Yankee"
neighbors provided a rough framework for understanding it.

Later in college (e.g. Bates College in Lewiston,
Maine) I began making some informal observations of
French language use in "public places." I conducted my
first semi-systematic study in 1958 when I concluded
that fifty percent of the conversations in the central
business district of Lewiston were in French.

Other experiences during this time provided "impressions" which were filed away, based on summer work
experiences and as a musician with entre into the in-
ner-sanctum of French clubs, weddings, and various
social events. During this time, close personal rela-
tionships with local French musicians provided a closer
look at French culture, values, thought, and patterns
of behavior.

It was only in 1961 as a graduate student in
Sociology at the University of Iowa, that I began put-
ting down some of my observations on paper, including
an organizational analysis of the French Culture Movement. By 1965 it became apparent that by pure luck I
had stumbled upon a very interesting cultural process
and quite by accident, had the background and data to
document it. The process I am speaking of, was a sudden decline in French language and culture during the
1960's in Lewiston. In less than ten years, French
culture and organization had broken down, and the
French people had been assimilated into mainstream
"Yankee" culture.

Over a period of 24 years, beginning in 1958, this
project has gone from a small survey of French language
use, and a few notes and impressions regarding culture
and organization to an expanded treatment found in this
book. As it now stands, six methodologies are fused
into this study, all of which point in the same general
direction. Rarely do findings, using a variety of
methods fit together so nicely. Here, we found that

historical data, government documents, survey data, cultural analysis, organizational analysis, and participant observation complemented each other with a minimum of distortion of results.

The general thrust of the book as it has developed, centers around the documentation of a case of cataclysmic cultural breakdown. Drawing upon many types of data, an attempt has been made to show that the French-American culture suffered an abrupt, multigenerational shift in cultural and social orientation. This alone justifies the study. Beyond this, however, a number of other related considerations bearing on this general problem were examined.

One problem that arose, was why this particular culture at this particular time, disintegrated so abruptly. In order to answer this question a large portion of the book deals with the bifurcated nature of French culture and its resultant consequences for cultural breakdown. Specifically we were interested in the development of a "real" and an "ideal" French culture. The "real" culture being more "humanistic" and need oriented, and the "ideal" culture resembling the "puritanical" Yankee culture.

Rather than recapitulate the entire argument and analysis at this point, it seems more proper to allow the full story to unfold in the remaining pages at a more leisurely pace.

With this brief introduction let me thank several persons and organizations for their contribution to this endeavor. First, I would like to express my appreciation to Andrea Gauthier, Leo Pepin, and other Lewiston-Auburn friends for their contribution to my understanding of French and "Yankee" cultures. My brother-in-law, William Bartley, himself of French descent, and my sister Nancy Bartley were a great help in collecting and providing information. Also Gary Rugendorf deserves special thanks for his direction of the Attitude Survey in 1972. The study would have been less complete except for the cooperation of the Androscoggin Historical Society, The Lewiston Public Library, the people at the Lewiston Model Cities Office and Professor Thomas Stirton's critical evaluation of the final draft. Finally, my father, Donald F. Parker, is most responsible for my continuing interest in French culture, by providing stimulating intellectual discussions over the years on all the problems treated in this book.

Chapter 1

The French in Maine: Beginnings

The city of Lewiston is located in Southern Maine about fifteen miles from the seacoast and about 150 miles north of Boston. Directly across the Androscoggin River is its sister city Auburn. These two cities and contiguous built up areas comprise the second largest metropolitan area in Maine. The size of this metro area is about 100,000 people. Lewiston has approximately 40,000 population and Auburn has 25,000. (U.S. Bureau of the Census, 1972).

The history of Lewiston begins when the area was still a part of Massachusetts.

> "Paul Hildreth moved into the plantation of 'Lewiston' in the autumn of 1770. He built his log cabin on the bank of the river just below the Continental Mill . . . Tradition relates many adventures experienced during the early settlement of the place, of marvelous contests with venomous wild beasts which invaded the sanctity of the settlement; of women frightened; of children pursued by bears; of the destruction of cattle by huge and ferocious catamounts; of the dread experienced as the dusky forms of the aborigines were seen gliding through the forests in pursuit of game . . . The pioneers' life was a sad and checkered reality. A trackless forest, fifteen miles in extent, lay between them and the nearest white settlement." (Merrill, p. 345)

The city experienced very gradual growth until just prior to the Civil War.

> "In 1770 Lewiston had 532 inhabitants . . . in 1800 the population was 948; 1810, 1,038; 1820, 1,312; 1840, 1,810. From 1840 there has been a wondrous growth, keeping pace with the increase in manufacturing. In March, 1848, the Androscoggin and Kennebec Railroad was completed as far as Lewiston . . ." (Merrill, pp. 351-352)

1

The ethnic background of the population up to the Civil War in the city of Lewiston was predominantly English and Scotch. Some of the names mentioned as historical figures at this time confirm this. Such names as these keep cropping up: Ames, Garcelon, Merrill, Morrell, Thompson, Davis, Robinson, Barker, Fields, Blaisdell, Wright, Frye, Ham, Parker, Crowley, etc. (Merrill, pp. 351-352)

The opening of textile mills driven by abundant water power from the Androscoggin River gave Lewiston its economic base for the next 100 years of its growth and was probably the most crucial series of events in the history of the city. The textile mills began operation in the following order: (Merrill, pp. 384-390)

Lewiston Falls Mfg. Co.	1819
First Cotton Fabric Mill	1836
Hill Mfg. Co.	1850
Bates Mfg. Co.	1852
Continental Mills	1858
Androscoggin Mill	1869

It was during this period (1830-1870) that French speaking <u>Canadiens</u> from Quebec, began migrating to the Lewiston area to work in the mills. Thus a change in economic base introduced ethnic diversity into the area for the first time.

These French-Canadiens were descendants of immigrants from France who had settled in Quebec Province in the 17th Century. As early as 1800 there were significant colonies of these Canadiens in Northern Maine. It was primarily poor economic conditions together with unusually high birth rate that caused large numbers of French to move to New England. (Michaud: 1971a)

French occupation of Maine was much earlier than this, however. Apparently the first European settlement in Maine was started on an island in the St. Croix River by French colonists in 1604. In 1752 French Huguenots (Protestants) settled in what is now the town of Dresden. In 1785 when Northern Maine was still an unsettled frontier a small group of French pioneers traveled from Fredericton, New Brunswick, and settled Madawaska, Maine. As early as 1827 the first French (Canadien) immigrants settled in Waterville. By 1831 Lewiston had 30 French families. Vicero (1968) estimates that French Canada experienced a net loss of 600,000 persons to New England between 1840 and 1900,

2

about four-fifths after 1860. In 1900 Massachusetts had nearly half the entire Franco-American population, Southern Maine and New Hampshire sharing another quarter about equally, (Vicero). In Maine several cities had a sizeable percentage of French population such as Biddeford (62%), Lewiston (46%), Waterville (45%), Brunswick (54%), and Old Town (52%), (Vicero). Accordint to Allen (1970), Lewiston's French population increased fifteen percent since that time making that city sixty-one percent French. This figure, however, is entirely unreliable given the analysis of the Lewiston City Directory, 1970-71 (H.A. Manning Co.) by this investigator. Our analysis found seventy-eight percent of the surnames listed in the Directory were French. If we assume that two percent of French names have been anglicized, which is probably the case, we may conclude that four-fifths of Lewiston's population is French at this time. It is entirely probable that Lewiston has the highest proportion of French-Americans of any sizeable city in the United States. It is also likely that the French in this city were the most successful for the longest period of time in maintaining their French language and culture in a metro area.

Many of the cultural characteristics of French Canada shed some light on the adaptations made by the French in America. Life was hard in this primarily rural society in the 18th and 19th century. There were few industries to provide employment and most people were engaged in eking out a marginal income from farming. In spite of this the French were unusually fecund, with families of 12 children not being uncommon (Michaud: 1971b). In less than a century (1759-1851) the French population grew from 60,000 to 670,000 (Maine Historical Society: 1972, p. 9). Women often wove and made their own clothes, as well as helping out in the fields. Usually most owned their own homestead, however humble. Schools were non-existent in those early days and the parish priest was the intellectual, political, legal and moral authority in the community (Michaud: 1971b). A classic study of a French-Canadian community (Miner) shows that in St. Denis at least, the French community was a very equalitarian one with little variation in wealth and life style. The main exception to this was the existence of a very small elite made up of the local pastor and his family and the local Senator and his family. Like all communities there were a few at the bottom who were looked down upon partly because they violated community values and norms. There also appeared to be social

3

organization along the lines of extended families and to some extent, neighborhoods. It was a very familistic and ecclesiastic community with the extended family being the basic unit of the society and the church, and in particular the parish priest, furnishing the basis of wider community integration. Social mobility appears not to have been a primary or even very important goal in the French-Canadian culture. Hughes (1943) as well as Miner (1939) substantiates this view. It was, in any case, a highly stable and integrated culture.

For our purposes these themes of French-Canadian culture had important effects on the French cultural adaptation in given education and social mobility, familism, cultural stability, and experience in textiles.

When the French went to work and live in Lewiston and other parts of New England, they brough with them these cultural characteristics which shaped their life style and community organization. One obvious parallel is that they shifted from home production of textiles which had been carried on for many generations in Canada for domestic consumption to being gainfully employed in large mass-production textile mills in the U.S. Also for centuries French-Canadians had been woodsmen at home in the vast tracts of virgin forest, a few as Voyageurs and many lumbermen, throughout the United States and Canada. In Maine, especially Northern Maine, many took up the occupation of tree cutters and lumbermen either as a full time job or as an adjunct winter occupation to supplement farming (Michaud: 1971a).

However varied the French-Canadians' occupations were in Maine in the early days, their primary occupations in Lewiston in the 19th century were working in the "new" mass production textile mills and the neighboring city of Auburn. Their experience in handicraft cottage industry in Canada also prepared them for work in the shoe factories. Work was long and hard and the pay was low in these mills and shops. Conditions were comparable to the early days of the industrial revolution in England, and to the hard country life in French-Canada. If deprivation and hard work prepares one for more deprivation, these French mill workers were well prepared. Hamon (1891) describes the conditions in these mills in much the same way as this investigator's own great grandfather did:

4

"The noise was deafening, heat prostra-
tion was common. Cotton dust choked the lungs.
A high percentage of the workers developed eye
problems, especially women."

Franco-Americans did not hesitate to send their
children to work often at a very early age, which of
course was common practice at that time. At the turn
of the century, textile employees worked form 6:00 A.M.
to 6:00 P.M., for $2.00 a day or less, 60 hours a week
(Knowlton). The textile industry, even today, is one
of the most depressed, paying some of the lowest wages
in industry, and with weak, ineffective unions unable
to obtain significant benefits for their members.

Another cultural characteristic carried by the
French to Maine was a low level of mobility aspirations. A study conducted in Lewiston (Ritter) in 1969
indicated that even among the poorer French-Americans
there was little interest in further education, higher
degrees, better training, or even better housing. This
is in keeping with the observation by most sociologists
involved in the study of stratification that the
French-Canadian is the least socially mobile of white
ethnic groups in America. From this investigator's informal participation in the French community life a
possible explanation may be seen for this. The investigator's role in the French community was primarily
that of a musician which gained him entre into French
organizational and informal social life. This participation took place primarily during the 1950's in
Lewiston and Auburn, which included intimate contact
with a group of French musicians and their families
over an extended period of time. Several important
observations were made then. One observation was that
the French were seldom apologetic about their language
or culture. They, in fact, appeared proud of their
heritage and seemed to immensely enjoy their language,
culture, and fellow Frenchmen. In short, they highly
valued their culture and gained intrinsic satisfaction
from it, rather than using it as a means to extrinsic
ends. French life was looked at as the good life and
great emphasis was placed upon getting together with
other people of the same cultural background. French
culture was viewed as valuable in its own right and
appeared to satisfy needs for social acceptance,
social esteem, self esteem and personal growth unusually well, thus reducing motivation to seek a
"better" life. These factors, alone, go a long way
toward explaining the tenacity with which

5

French-Canadians everywhere in the United States have clung to their culture while other more recently arrived ethnic groups, like the Irish, moved up the social ladder.

Another cultural strand that was carried from French-Canada to Lewiston was the strong elements of familism, especially the extended family, and neighborhood social organization. (Michaud, 1971b) recounts how money was always borrowed from within the extended family. Extended family and neighborhood social events were frequent and spirited as evidenced by the following account (Michaud: 1971b):

> "After the children had gone to bed, in winter snug under heavy blankets in the unheated rooms, it was time for adults to socialize with talk and card games. They came from across the hall, upstairs and down, all from within the same "block", as the tenement houses were called. Card games were spirited affairs, marked with running commentary and good-humored banter; much laughter, and considerable slapping of cards on the table when there was an especially clever play . . . When tragedy struck a home, neighbors were quick to bring aid and comfort, not waiting to be asked."

This investigator's participant observation in the 1950's confirmed the important role that the extended family played in French-American culture. Observations at musical "jam sessions", picnics, and other "get to-gethers" revealed that there was usually two or three generations present, with each generation interested in, interacting with, and being equalitarian with, each other. The equalitarianism was very evident along with great respect paid to elders, and deep involvement and interest in the children. This mutual respect and involvement showed itself by the fact that subgroups very seldom formed along age lines and interaction was as frequent between generations as within them. A great deal of visiting between members of the extended family was also evident and when not visiting, frequent comments about missing members occurred. The The comments were almost always positive and little backbiting and gossip was observed. This solidarity, however, did not result in rigid lines drawn against outsiders. Outsiders, even non-French people, were

treated hospitably and in a friendly manner. It was
particularly striking how quickly an outsider was
accepted and made to feel welcome and important.

These social events also dramatized the importance
of "oral" activities in French culture. Although
"oral" is used as a stereotype of Frenchmen in popular
literature, it is nevertheless descriptive to some
extent. Talking, singing, eating, and drinking appeared to be important activities. Christmas celebrations,
for example, involved the (almost ritual) getting together in families, talking and eating "pork pie" on
Christmas Eve. Conversations at French social events
was incessant and animated, with much gesturing and
bodily movement. French culture in Lewiston was to
some extent a drinking culture, with Saturday nights
set aside for attendance at the many French "clubs" or
other places where one could drink, sing, and
converse with his friends. This "orality" showed
itself also in the general "receptivity" and "assimilation" of outsiders, although receptivity of foreign
ideas was at a minimum. There was not so much a
hostile rejection of foreign influences as a passive
ignoring of them. This ignoring took the form of not
hearing, not understanding, forgetting, or not attend-
int to foreign material. In psychoanalytic terms the
response was passive-aggressive. This same pattern of
response to threat was many times repeated in the
French Culture Movement which we will discuss later.
Over-all one noticed a rejection of ideas rather than
of persons. The movement mentioned above never at any
time condemned the "Yankees". Rather they took a
"live and let live" attitude toward them, and at the
same time took a rather positive view of their own
culture.

A number of other cultural traits were brought
from Quebec, forming a cluster which can be called the
humanistic ethic. These traits are all oriented
toward satisfaction of basic human needs or drives,
rather than toward a set of abstract rules. Some of
the traits observed include a consumption orientation,
or being oriented toward final end states (such as
eating, relating etc.), rather than treating activities
as means to other ends. Another trait is the orientation toward traditional authority (traditional folk-
ways) rather than bureaucratic, legalistic rules. In
fact, we might characterize French culture as it is
practiced as a folk rather than an urban culture. A
further trait of this culture complex is a collective

orientation (toward group goals) as opposed to a more individualistic orientation. A central facet of this culture complex is need orientation (fulfilling basic needs) as opposed to an ideational orientation (toward abstract formal rules). The social structure tends to be more equalitarian and cooperative than status striving or hierarchical. It also tends to be more hedonistic or pleasure oriented than stoic or pain oriented. Finally we find more of an expressive orientation (e.g. to express oneself) than an instrumental (treating activities as a means to an end) one.

In direct contrast to these traits were the culture traits of the environing Yankee culture in New England. This culture complex can best be described as puritanical. Self expression and uninhibitedness were not practiced widely. Pleasure was often viewed with suspicion as possibly being immoral, although not necessarily in religious terms. Drinking and gambling were taboo. Talking loudly or too frequently was considered in bad taste. Given the alternatives of expressing oneself or following a fairly rigid social code, the Yankees followed the code. Repression or suppression took precedence over expression. Work was not only a means to an end, but also an end in itself. It was better to keep one's suffering and joys to oneself, and after all suffering was pretty much what life was about and was to be quietly endured in a stoic fashion.

These cultural differences are summarized on Table 1.

Table 1
Culture Traits of French
and Yankees

French (Humanistic Ethic)	Yankee (Puritan Ethic)
1. Consumption oriented	Work oriented
2. Traditional authority	Legal-Rational Authority
3. Folk	Urban
4. Collective Orientation	Individualistic Orientation
5. Basic Need Orientation	Ideational
6. Equalitarian	Hierarchical
7. Pleasure Oriented	Stoic
8. Expressive Orientation	Instrumental Orientation

These cultural differences, however wide, never became the basis of cultural solidarity on the part of the French but did for the "English." Yankees often spoke about the loudness and excessive expressivity of the French and considered themselves superior in this light. The friendliness and openness of the French was considered pushiness and ignorance. Their "hard-work" was appreciated but their lack of mobility aspirations was viewed as further evidence of cultural inferiority. On the other hand, the French often compared themselves favorably to the "English" in Yankee terms. They would make reference to their religiousity, their civil obedience, their hard work, and even their long-suffering history in Canada. This habit of evaluating themselves in terms of Yankee values probably in the long run reduced their ethnic solidarity. This investigator does believe, however, that the French, even in Canada, had an "ideal" culture[*] strongly influenced by the Roman Catholic Church which happened to resemble "English" values. The "real" culture however, was decidedly different from the ideal. This tension between the real and the ideal seems to have pervaded French culture in North America and served to reduce their appreciation and understanding of the positive elements in their real culture which set them apart from the English and gave them a unique social life. At least this latent tendency toward puritanical values may have been one of the forces which eventually resulted in assimilation. In a sense the ideal culture began to gain ascendance over the real. Here is possibly one factor that can explain part of the breakdown in French culture. The question arises, however, why the ideal gained ascendancy over the real, and at that particular time (1960's). One thing we have already pointed out is the strong resemblance between Yankee "real" culture and French "ideal" culture. Both of these had strong puritanical and stoic elements, one carried out in practice and the others as an ideal. Generations of contact between these two cultures (French and Yankee) may well have served to reinforce "ideal" French culture at the expense of the real culture. On the other hand, there was nothing in the Yankee environing culture that would reinforce the "real" French culture.

To carry this analysis somewhat further we should point out that there is also a split, though less

*Note: French ideal culture, from this point on will be used to designate what the French thought their culture was about, and is comparable to the real Yankee puritanical culture.

9

radical than the French case, between Yankee real and ideal culture. The relationship is directly obverse to the French case. The Yankee ideal culture is some- what more humanistic than that carried out in practice. That is, he sees himself ideally as not being partic- ularly puritanical or religious. He, ideally, can have a good time and let go once in a while. He does not see himself as a prudish person or unfriendly. In fact his ideal conception of himself is one of being highly friendly, open and accepting. The relevance of all this for our argument is that at the same time that French culture was becoming more puritanical, Yankee culture was becoming more humanistic. It would be tempting to attribute this to the influence of the French, but there is no good evidence for such an in- terpretation. The more convincing argument is that the reinforcement for humanistic elements in Yankee ideal culture is the society wide trend in this direc- tion. One need not document this wider cultural trend since it seems so evident, except to point out the general relaxation of the work ethic, sexual standards, standards of dress, and a general atmosphere of per- missiveness which has grown during the past fifty years.

So we see a number of cross-currents in this community. First, French culture was leaning toward the old Yankee cultural values, and Yankee culture, somewhat more assimilated, was gravitating toward the trends of the wider society. It is probably also true that the French were also being influenced by wider societal trends.

From a functional view all this makes sense, especially with respect to social mobility. As a suppressed minority the French could use the old ideal culture as a vehicle for social mobility, since these values are conducive to such mobility. The Yankees, on the other hand, could use some of the new societal ethic to allow them to enjoy the fruits of their past mobility.

One additional problem needs to be examined here. Why, or under what conditions did the French develop a bifurcated culture while in French Canada? The in- fluence of English culture is undoubtedly of some im- portance. However, the life conditions of the French in Quebec is, perhaps, a better jumping off place. As we have noted, life in French Canada in the 17th, 18th and 19th centuries was extremely harsh. The death rate was very high, food and good land was scarce, and existence was generally precarious. Under these conditions religion often comes to play an important part in a culture. It may serve as a substitute gratification, or serve to justify and explain suffering and rigorous standards of life. In short, religion often sustains an ideology of deprivation and stoicism. This was perhaps the case in French-Canada, at least our knowledge of the influence and teaching of the Church sustains this interpretation. The ideal French-Canadian culture, then, may have been born of suffering. The "real" or humanistic elements of French culture seems to correspond more to what we know of French culture in Europe. Thus we may surmise that this may have been the source of the "real" culture of French-Canadians. At least it can be traced to such a source. Thus we find the French developing two opposing reactions to deprivation; one stoic, religious and other worldly, and the other expressive, hedonistic, and social.

In any case these are some of the ingredients of French culture in the New World that may explain some of the cultural adaptations in Lewiston.

Equalitarianism survived in French culture as it made the transition from French-Canada to Maine. The great majority of French in Lewiston lived at about the same class level and may be described as working class. This undoubtedly contributed to the great solidarity exhibited by this ethnic group for over one hundred years. However, as Brault points out (Maine Historical Society), even very early a business and professional elite developed which tended to be somewhat more assimilated but paradoxically later formed the leadership of the French Culture Movement. Never-the-less there does not seem to have been deep class divisions within the community.

The housing patterns changed radically when the French moved from Quebec to New England milltowns. Instead of living in detached farmsteads they were now thrown together into "Little Canada", living in tenements near the mills. An example of these housing conditions is Little Canada in Lewiston which still exists today. Located near the river and mills, 26 percent of the city's population is contained on 1.5 percent of the land (Reilly). The borders of Little Canada are the Androscoggin River, Cedar and Lincoln Streets. Most of the tenements are four or five stories high and were built in the 19th century. The foul odor of the Androscoggin River, due to sulfite wastes from paper mills upriver, permeate the crowded neighborhood. Some of its streets are too narrow for two cars to easily pass one another. It resembles the Little Italys and old ethnic neighborhoods throughout our major cities. Excerpts from an article on Little Canada in the Maine Times (Reilly) give some flavor of the neighborhood:

> "The architecture and the language are of the past. Oxford and River Streets are incredibly narrow - the much venerated alleys of Quebec City come to mind. The wooden tenements are built nearly on top of one another, sometimes separated by only a two or three foot alley . . . . Janelle (a community leader) who came to Lewiston in 1896 to settle on Knox Street in another French neighborhood, remembers French stores and bakeries, French plays, concerts, and lectures. He even remembers swimming and drinking from the Androscoggin River and admits much of this has changed now. . . They called Little Canada "The Island" then and it still is today. It is an island teeming with life and surrounded with decaying buildings for rent or sale, vacant lots, gap-eyed brick mills with space for rent, and streets congested with traffic. . . On its backside is the river topped with brown swirls of chemical whipped cream."

The important fact for our purposes, however is the dense housing pattern had the function of maintaining French culture. High density apparently fit rather well with the "social" proclivities of the French even though they had not lived in this kind of housing before. It also provided protection against assimilation, as all ghettos do, by providing a complete way of life in a small area, blocked off from other influences. In general the poorer French population lived nearer the river and the mills, and the housing became better as one moved out from the river. It is probably true that distance from the river is a rough measure of assimilation and recency of migration.

Even in Little Canada, however, the majority of people now speak mainly English (Reilly).

The pivotal role of the church was transplanted from Canada to Lewiston, also. The first complete Franco-American parochial school in Maine and the third in New England was founded by the Grey Nuns in Lewiston in 1878 (Paroisse Saint-Pierre et Saint-Paul, pp. 22-31). The Ursuline Sisters arrived in Lewiston in 1916 and built schools (Maine Historical Society, p. 20). It was the Dominican Fathers, who arrived in 1881, that made the greatest educational impact. They opened an elementary French parochial shool in Lewiston in 1883 (Paroisse Saint-Pierre et Saint-Paul, pp. 22-31), and established the first regional French Catholic High School in Lewiston in 1941 (St. Dominics High School), (Paroisse . . . p. XXX). These schools, supported by the Church, provided several very important functions for the French community, not the least of which was to maintain the French language. Others of its latent functions was to teach French-Canadian history, provide a common cultural background for French children, and to propagate French Catholic values. It was also through these schools that the clergy could exercise maximum influence on developing young minds, inculcating the "ideal" French culture. If a French student wished to continue his education in French parochial schools, he could attend Assumption College in Worchester, Massachusetts, or attend college in Quebec. On the whole, though, the French were not particularly interested in higher education. Even in the 1960's only a small proportion of French students attended college. It was not unusual for French politicians to make speeches about the lack of necessity to have much formal schooling when a bond issue came up. This investigator recalls in the fifties a French mayor of limited education, making the statement that he had only an elementary school education and had done alright so why couldn't other people do the same. This lack of interest in education was probably one cause of the lack of social mobility in the French population. Even if they had wanted to, limited education would have prevented most from rising on the social ladder. This lack of interest in education, especially liberal education, has its roots in Quebec where only a technical, professional, or theological education was generally considered useful (Hughes). A survey of the model cities neighborhoods in 1969 indicates that this lack of interest in education continues. When asked to mention the "most important city problem" only 1.6 percent mentioned the need to improve education. Less than one half of one percent listed it as the most serious neighborhood

13

problem (Ritter: pp. 3.4 and 3.8). When asked if anybody in the family will go on for college, only 13 percent answered "yes" (Ritter: p. 3.41). Although this was a low status sample, college aspirations seem abnormally low.

The role of the priest in the French community in Canada was crucial and important. This same situation existed in Lewiston for many years, and even today the priest is an important figure in the community. Michaud (1971b) sums up the priest's role in the early days of French migration:

> "It was common practice then to look to the parish priest and his assistants for aid of all kinds. The parish priest was the counselor on all matters temporal and spiritual. He visited his parishoners in their homes, was acquainted with all their problems, and served as lawyer, architect, doctor, and what-not, as attested in early parish records. The parish priest even served as banker for many of these early residents. Distrustful of strangers and unacquainted with English-speaking citizens, they did business only among their own."

Again, the Priest as a representative of the Church reinforced and propagated the "ideal" culture of the French community.

* * *

We have tried to present here, the cultural elements that were inherited from French-Canada which made up, to a large extent, the French adaptation to Lewiston. It should aid us in understanding later developments in the French community as they sought to maintain their language and culture.

It should be pointed out, however, that some degree of acculturation was taking place constantly during the 19th and 20th centuries. English expressions crept into the language, some mobility occurred, and English was learned by most of the community. Even intermarriage occurred to some extent. No doubt in other subtle ways their culture changed during this period, but it would be difficult to document such changes.

Our next step is to document how, in the early 20th century, the French consolidated their social organization in a new setting, and developed a set of organizations and practices serving to maintain and hopefully to spread their culture.

Chapter 2

Consolidation of French Culture

The population of Lewiston grew steadily as Table 2 indicates, until it reached 41,000 in 1970.

Table 2

Population of Lewiston 1860-1970

Year	Population	Reference
1860	7,424	(Kennedy)
1870	13,600	(U.S. Dept. of the Interior)
1880	19,083	(U.S. Dept. of the Interior)
1890	21,701	(U.S. Census Office)
1900	23,761	(U.S. Census Office)
1910	26,247	(U.S. Bureau of the Census, 1931)
1920	31,971	(U.S. Bureau of the Census, 1931)
1930	34,948	(U.S. Bureau of the Census, 1931)
1940	38,598	(U.S. Bureau of the Census, 1961)
1950	40,974	(U.S. Bureau of the Census, 1961)
1960	40,804	(U.S. Bureau of the Census, 1961)
1970	41,779	(U.S. Bureau of the Census, 1972)

The increase of the French population as a percentage of the total population is a more difficult figure to arrive at. Le Messager (1961b) gives figures up to 1875 which are presented in Table 3.

Table 3

The Growth of the French Population in Lewiston

Year	French Population
1869	1,000
1872	1,500
1875	2,896

According to this, the French population was about 19 percent of the total in 1875, which roughly coincides with the founding of the first French church. Earlier we cited data which indicated that as early as 1831 there were thirty French families in Lewiston.

As we have mentioned, an analysis of the Lewiston City Directory, 1970-1971 by this investigator revealed that the percentage of French now is 80 percent (32,000 people). The growth of the French population

17

between 1875 and 1970, however, will have to be estimated from the data that we have. Table 4 (Lemaire 1966) based on census data suggests that the great influx was just about completed by 1910, although thereafter there was some increase in the number of French foreign-born in Maine.

Table 4

Foreign Born in Maine Claiming French

Mother Tongue

Year	Foreign Born Population Claiming French Mother Tongue
1910	35,342
1920	36,071
1930	37,325
1940	29,140
1960	21,091

Our estimate would be that the French constituted over 50 percent of the population by 1910. The fact that a French Mayor was elected in 1914 suggests that the French constituted more than a majority of the population. Given the problems of organizing a political power base, it is likely that our date of 1910 as the shifting of majorities period is roughly correct or even a little late. Also we would estimate from this that the majority of French people in Lewiston migrated prior to 1900 which would make the average French resident in Lewiston 4th or 5th generation American (counting immigrants as 1st generation). In other words the average French family in the city have been there for over 70 years. They are, then, hardly newcomers. In fact, based on Le Messager figures (see Table 3), we would estimate that fully 20 percent of all French families have been there for 100 years or more.

Thus, we are not dealing with a new immigrant group but, virtually, old settlers. It is interesting that an ethnic group could maintain its language and culture for such a long period without experiencing significant acculturation. This point cannot be made too strongly. It is important to understand and appreciate the cultural stability of this group. This is a rare achievement for an urban ethnic group in the United States. The only groups that approximate such an achievement are the Amish in Pennsylvania and Iowa, and groups of American Indians. These exceptions,

18

however, are groups which isolated themselves geograph-
ically and followed a rural way of life.

Cultural Milieu

The sources of potential conflict between the
French and the surrounding Yankee population are
obvious. First, the French were Roman Catholic, spoke
French, were usually rural in background, and were
generally lower in occupational status than the
Yankees. The Yankees, on the other hand, were Protest-
ant, spoke English, were urbanized, and had a higher
occupational status.

Several factors, however, tended to mitigate con-
flicts between the two groups. The "ideal" French-
Canadian culture embodied many cherished values of the
New England Yankee, such as piety, civil obedience,
family solidarity and hard work. Finally, occupational
differences between the French and Yankees which could
have been a source of conflict turned out to be a more
complementary relationship with the French working
largely as laborers and the Yankees more frequently
being managers, professionals, and service workers.
Everett Hughes (1943) notes this same division of
labor in a city in Quebec Province. This is not to
say, however, that no class conflict existed between
the two groups. Overt expressions of class and cultural conflict, though, usually took the form of language conflict, or a suspicion of each other's
religions. The Yankees could not understand why the
French would not speak English and the French could
not understand what was wrong with speaking French.
The Yankee's recurrent complaint was that the French
would not speak English, or that they did not speak
good English. There is no evidence that the Yankees
consciously used their power as managers, owners and
professionals to coerce the French into speaking
English. However, since English speaking people con-
trolled and managed most of the large industries, there
were undoubtedly organizational pressures for the use
of English. Conflict about language usage usually
took the form of banter and mild ridicule about language differences. The Yankees among themselves often
imitated the broken English used by the French.

The divergent values of the two cultures, however,
never were made public issues, nor were they the subject of much conversation between the two groups.

The Growth of French Organization

The French, although they had been in Lewiston since the early 1800's did not, to our knowledge, develop formal organizations until the founding of the first French Church in 1870 (see Table 5).

Table 5

The Founding of Various French Culture Groups in Lewiston (Le Messager, 1961a)

Name of Group*	Date of Founding
First French Church	1870
Institute Jacques Cartier	1872
La Theatre Franco-Americaine	1899
L'Orpheon Societe	1912
Le Montagnard	1923
Club Jacques Cartier	1925
La Chorale De Lewiston	1927
Le Club Musical	1940
L'Union Americaine Des Raquetteurs	1941

The Institute Jacques Cartier was founded soon after in 1872. A French theatre group was formed in 1899. A number of organizations appeared in the early part of the 20th century soon after the great migration from Canada. Among them was a choral group, a music club, and a social club. By 1960, however, 29 French formal organizations had developed.

The most surprising thing about these developments is the slowness with which formal organizations developed in this community. Prior to 1910 there were only a few such organizations, although half the population was French. Also, these organizations tended to be expressive rather than instrumental organizations. One would expect that, given the pressing social needs of a new immigrant community, more social welfare organizations would have developed. The lack of experience and familiarity of the French in Canada with formal organizations is perhaps one reason for

*Note: To my knowledge there were no earlier organizations than these. These organizations (listed) were still functioning in 1961, but later underwent alterations making them less ethnic. This will be discussed later.

this. A second even more important reason may be that the Church had always been the social service agency in the French community and that the French population had come to rely on it. It is probably true that even in Lewiston, the Church and church-related organizations provided most of the early organizational structure.

Political Organization

An indication of growing organizational effectiveness and complexity in the French community is the history of Mayors in Lewiston. Table 6 indicates that there were a large number of French Mayors beginning with 1914 until 1932. Since 1932 until 1970 all Lewiston Mayors were French. All told, from 1914 until 1971, 49 out of 57 Mayors have been French. By 1932 the French were, in effect, in political control of the city.

Table 6[*]

History of Mayors in Lewiston

Year	Non-French	French
1914		1
1915	1	
1916	1	
1917-1920		4
1921-1924	4	
1925-1929		5
1930-1931	2	
1932-1970		39

[*]Data compiled from Le Messager, Sept. 14, 1961 and from Lewiston City Clerk's Records.

Table 7 shows the degree of that control by 1961. All the State Senators and Representatives from Lewiston, all County Commissioners and other elected county officials, and all but two city councilmen were French in 1961.

21

Table 7

Political Offices Held by French
in 1961 (Le Messager, 1961b)

Offices	Total	No. Held By French
State		
State Senators from Lewiston	3	3
State Representatives from Lewiston	6	6
County (Androscoggin)		
County Commissioners	3	3
Other Elective Posts	4	4
Municipal (Lewiston)		
Mayor	1	1
Councilmen	7	5

The Movement

By 1960 a powerful and extensive social movement had developed in Lewiston, which we will call the French Culture Movement. Briefly, this movement had as its purpose the preservation of French culture, not only in Lewiston, but in all of New England where large enclaves of French-Canadians lived. It is our purpose here, to examine the movement in detail, showing its aims, tactics, ideology and organizational structure. This analysis should illustrate the nature of French culture and demonstrate the ethnic solidarity, involvement and intensity that had developed.

Why a social movement should have developed is a difficult question to answer. French was still widely spoken by the French community and the parochial school system was healthy. But, there may well have been strong anxieties about the viability of French culture in Lewiston. The decline in readership of the only French newspaper and the growing popularity of English television may have been sufficient warning for French leaders to develop a counter-attack. Also as early as the fifties some school-aged French children were showing a preference for English. The intermarriage rate with Yankees was also rising.

The ethnic community was more or less intact in the late fifties, however. Informal observations by this investigator, for example, during 1958 showed that about 50 percent of the conversations in the central business district were in French. A retrospective study conducted among merchants in 1973 (to be more fully explained later) confirms this estimate. As we will demonstrate, the organizational structure of the French community was also intact at this time.

An analysis of the movement reveals interesting facets of French thought and culture and demonstrates the ethnic cohesion and involvement that existed at that time. As might be expected, the movement had close ties with the Church and in turn was supported by the Church, at least in Lewiston. The Diocese itself, however, and the national hierarchy, dominated by Irish clerics took a dim view of ethnic churches and ethnic preservation movements. Their policy in general was to assimilate Catholics into mainstream American culture.

The clergy in Lewiston, however, was mainly French-Canadian, spoke French, and shared French values. It was for this reason, and probably because of parish pressure, that the local Catholic clergy supported the movement. Through the Catholic schools and the church services themselves, the use of French language was encouraged and propagated. Perhaps more important, the Church served to legitimize the use of French language and to make it normatively prescriptive.

The movement also revealed a newly developed penchant for joining formal organizations among the French. In Quebec there was no strong tendency in this direction, and if anything the French there preferred informal social interaction. In Lewiston from 1930 to 1960 a plethora of formal organizations came into being.

The movement also revealed the importance of the somewhat latent "ideal" culture which had its roots in French-Canada. The movement did not espouse friendliness, openness, and fun, but rather religiousity, hard work, and puritan values. Little was said about values of the "real," everyday, ongoing culture which stressed a more fun-loving, sociable, and humanistic orientation. The reason these values were not stressed is perhaps because they sound less noble and justifiable. It may be, on the other hand, an accurate representation of how the French viewed themselves. This investigator's field experience would lead him to believe that the latter is the case.

The movement also revealed the "live and let live"
philosophy of the French. They did not call for adop-
tion of their values by others, in general, but merely
encouraged their own people to practice and develop
their culture. Their lack of "out-group" hostility
also manifested itself in this movement. No reference
was made to the "bad" people outside French culture or
the oppressive environing culture of the Yankees.

Insight into French thinking is also gleaned by
noting the kinds of tactics the movement adopted. No
hostile or aggressive tactics such as strikes, demon-
strations, or hate campaigns were mentioned or conducted. Their tactics were non-destructive, non-
aggressive policies oriented toward changing themselves rather than others. They advocated such
innocuous things as more participation in French culture, more speaking of French, and more frequent visits
to Quebec.

Their organizational structure further reveals
their value system. There was no hint of invidious
stratification either within or between French organizations. These organizations appeared to be exception-
ally equalitarian with a minimum of hierarchy. These
organizations were generally expressive rather than
instrumental in orientation. This latter characteristic is most revealing, for French culture in general
appears to have been expressive and consumatory in
orientation even in Quebec.

Activism in the radical sense was missing from
the movement. It called for no heroics or dramatic
action, but merely called for continuing the tradition
of the past. This lack of dramatic or forceful action
also seemed to be a characteristic of the entire
culture.

The complexity of organization that developed in
the movement, however, was something new, not found in
rural Canada. The number of organizations mushroomed
and resembled interlocking directorates in their overlap of leadership and membership. Several institution-
al areas, such as political, religious, recreational,
and artistic were integrated through this overlapping
membership. A second principle of organization, aside
from overlapping membership, was that of redundancy.
It was never left to chance that one organization would
get the job done. Numbers of organizations were
created which repeated the function of others. This

was especially true of the "social" clubs, which had a primary function of maintaining French culture and solidarity. This redundancy and overlap resulted in an organizational fabric that covered New England and Canada. Super organizations (e.g. The League of French Language Societies) that attempted to integrate efforts of many smaller organizations spread over two (and if we count France, three) countries. But again redundancy was the organizing principle, not hierarchy, authority, or bureaucracy. Perhaps this was the only kind of organization that could develop in an equalitarian culture where the ideas of bureaucracy and hierarchy were foreign except in church organization. This flat, redundant organizational structure perhaps was one reason that the movement failed so abruptly. It was, perhaps, no match for the bureaucratic, powerful and instrumental organizations of the environing culture.

The Movement as a Reflection of the Nature of French Culture

We may state the general orientation of the French Culture Movement as being the conservation, development and diffusion of French Language and culture in the United States. The League of French Language Societies stated its aim "to spread and develop the French culture in this country," (Le Messager, 1961a).

More specifically, the goals of the movement as stated by "The League" were to promote the Catholic Church, promote the social and economic interests of French-Americans, encourage the use of French language, and to spread French culture in the United States (Le Messager, 1961a). One society, The Institute Jacques Cartier, stated its goals as "Working to maintain our religion, our language, and our traditions" (Le Messager, 1961b, p. 13). La Societe L'Assumption took a somewhat different line, stating its goals as "Insurance-Education-Social Action" (Le Messager, 1961b, p. 13).

If we order these goals according to the emphasis they receive in statements of ideology, we arrive at the following:

1. Maintaining the French language
2. Supporting the Catholic Church
3. Preserving other elements of French culture
4. Improving the Socio-Economic Status of
     Franco-Americans

The priority of these goals indicate that the main thrust of the movement was preservation of French language, religion and culture, not socio-economic upgrading, reducing prejudice, or proselytizing. Although proselytizing was expressed periodically as a goal of the league, nowhere in practice do we find evidence for it. This goal seems more like wishful thinking than a realistic objective. There were, however, reasons for the French to feel optimistic about " "spreading" their culture. The dominance and pervasiveness of French culture in Lewiston and neighboring cities gave the French an exaggerated estimate of the power and appeal of their way of life. Also, the close proximity of the parent culture in Quebec provided reinforcement of French culture and encouragement. Their great success in Canada and the United States in preserving their culture, undoubtedly was a factor. Perhaps most important was the positive way in which they viewed their culture, and their conviction that it was superior in many ways to mainstream American culture.

Their "defense doctrine," or ideological support of their goals centers mainly around the idea of the intrinsic superiority of their culture as evidenced by their outstanding record as U.S. citizens and their morally superior way of life. To quote briefly from Le Messager (1961a, p. 4):

> Everywhere in America our speech
> and our acts have been a living testimony
> of the excellence of our religion, of the
> superiority of our civilization, of which
> the language is both the product and the
> buttress . . . They (French) are the best
> Catholics in America, and also being
> Catholics are the best sons of the race
> and of the French civilization. Of
> necessity the French-Canadian became
> synonymous with honor, perserverance,
> courage, and dignity . . ."

One notes at this point the reference to "ideal" French cultural values rather that the "real" culture. Throughout their ideology, are references to this puritanical, stoic side of French culture, but no reference to the humanistic side of it, or the "real" culture. We also note the position of cultural superiority by this writer. This same kind of attitude, was sometimes encountered by this investigator in his

26

field work. French people periodically made statements about their language or religion which to non-French ears sounded ethnocentric. The intention behind these statements appeared to be that of positive cultural identification rather than any desire to humiliate or deflate the observer. It is curious in this vein to observe two more opposing tendencies in French culture and personality. One, we have just mentioned, are feelings of pride which appeared to be a minor tendency. The second, and opposing tendency, was to express (and I believe to feel) a sense of easy acceptance and un-self consciousness about their culture. This, at times, took the form of humility and good-humoredness. The latter sometimes shaded off into some feelings of inferiority which were expressed in very subtle ways, like apologies for poor English or explaining at length why the French act as they do. Again, the expressions of inferiority tended to be a minor tendency. The major thrust of French culture in this vein seemed to be the good-humored acceptance of their way of life. This split in French culture and personality seems to parallel the split we spoke of earlier, between the ideal and real culture. The ideal culture sustained by the church, produced feelings of excessive pride and assertiveness but at the same time results in feelings of inferiority, of not having lived up to their ideals. The "real" culture, on the other hand, is reflected in their easy-going acceptance of, and liking for their culture which is non-aggressive and positive.

While there was little direct criticism of other groups, criticism was directed toward the French themselves for neglecting their culture. Again, we sense their feeling that they have not quite lived up to their very high ideals. Even this criticism is muted and takes the form of advice and counseling. Again, we quote from Le Messager (1961b, p. 6):

"In order to love one's country one must learn about its geography, history, and the biographies of its great men. Learn the history of the United States well, for it is the country where you live, but do not neglect that of Canada . . . In becoming acquainted with the beauty and grandeur of the lives of your ancestors, you will understand what you owe to them and the direction you must, yourself, go in.

Especially, speak French in your
family so that your parents will not be
forced to impose this duty of primary
importance on you. In giving this advice
I am not afraid that you will not learn
English. English penetrates you from the
air you breathe because every hour of the
day it is made to ring in your ears.
Do your reading in French . . . The
beautiful stories are not necessarily all
written in English, and you will find them
other places than the magazines or big
American newspapers, which are often not
meant for you . . ."

One notes here the importance of identification
with French-Canada in the movement. Although careful
not to appear un-American, loyalty to Canada was
stressed.

All movements and cultures must have myths or
heroic models to anchor their ideology. This movement
had several myths and models which served to link
religion to French culture and promote solidarity within the French group. One hero, St. Jean Baptiste, is
the patron Saint of Quebec and provides the basis of
an ethnic holiday in Lewiston. Perhaps the most
important myth is the "myth of French survival in the
new world," providing as it does, a heroic historical
image of the French ethnic group. The myth centers
around an image of a group of Frenchmen surviving in a
hostile environment.

Out of this matrix of beliefs and hopes were
developed definite tactics and policies by which the
goals of the movement could be accomplished. These
tactics and policies mirror the French-Canadian pattern
of thought and action and offer considerable insight
into the French culture in Lewiston. The over-all
policies were modest and consisted of insulating the
French population from Anglo-American influences,
encouraging participation in purely French activities,
and gaining the appreciation of Anglo-Americans.
(Le Messager, 1961a).

The specific tactics of the movement varied considerably. One main tactic was to support parochial
education which in turn served to propagate the French
language and French ideal culture. The pivotal position of this approach was cogently expressed in

Le Messager (1961b, p. 6):

"Parochial students and schools
have been the fortress which defends
our language and our faith."

The use of mass media to develop and spread
French culture was also urged, along with the development
of credit unions, scholarships, insurance societies,
and business loans (Le Messager, 1961a and
1961b). Political action was never mentioned in the
ideology but it is evident that this was one main tactic
of the movement. However, the greatest contribution
of the political machine seems to have been a low
tax rate and loss of industry (Guignard).[*]

The scope of the movement was, then, very general
and the tactics rather vague and indefinite. It was
never made clear as to how one supports parochial
education, participates in French culture, or sets up
social welfare programs. To the investigator's knowledge
these tactics were never made more specific and
operational. They remained more as a general guideline
rather than precise rules for behavior.

This lack of specificity was typical of French
culture which seemed to serve more as a diffuse orientation
rather than as a set of specific role prescriptions.
French social functions in which the investigator
participated had this quality of diffuseness
and lack of planning. Spontaneity and autonomous behavior
seemed more typical than pre-planned formality.
The formalistic element in French society seemed
largely confined to church organization. It is little
wonder, then, that the movement had a certain ad hoc
quality about it. In terms of Parson's (1951) pattern
variables both the culture as a whole and the movement
itself had a small community quality to it. Taking
the pattern variables one at a time we find that the
culture (and the movement) had a diffuse rather than
a specific orientation, was particularistic rather than
universalistic, was affective rather than affectively

[*]Note: The French-controlled political machine contributed
to the loss of industry, essentially by taking
little action to prevent it. This again reflects
French values of acceptance of what seemed to be the
inevitable and their non-confrontational approach to
problems at every level.

neutral, tended to be based on ascription rather than achievement, and was more collectively oriented than self oriented. These are exactly the characteristics that describe a small, intimate, pre-industrial community.

By way of comparison, the Yankees were almost opposite in terms of the pattern variables. They tended to be universalistic, achievement oriented, affectively neutral, self oriented, and with a specificity of role expectations. These are characteristics of an urban, industrialized community.

Thus the French culture and the movement was a small town community challenging an urban community. One being primarily a rural cultural orientation and the other urban-industrialized. This may account, perhaps, in part for the later failure of the movement. What the movement was essentially trying to do was to maintain a "rural" form of social organization in the face of a urban-industrial, environing social organization.

Recruitment to the movement consisted mainly of interesting the French in their own culture and its organizational life. Little attempt was made to recruit non-French members, in fact some organizations restricted their membership to French people. Intermarriage did not usually result in recruitment of new members. The usual outcome was for the French member of the family and the children to become anglicized. So, in effect, intermarriage led to cultural attrition rather than recruitment.

The solidarity of the movement was insured by the common language, religion and cultural practices of its members. Institutionally, the Church, parochial schools and French voluntary associations provided a framework for the maintenance and expression of solidarity.

The organizational structure of the movement was composed of many, relatively small and loosely organized voluntary associations together with the formal apparatus of the Church. These smaller voluntary associations and a number of Church organizations (i.e. Ligue Du Sacre-Coeur, Ligue Du St. Nom) were loosely related to a central coordinating organization called the League of French Language Societies. This league apparently served as the integrating formal apparatus of the movement itself. Table 8 lists the variety of organizations formally affiliated with the League, both in Lewiston, and in other cities in Maine. The concentration of organizations in Lewiston as well as the fact that the central office of the League was there, suggests that Lewiston was the central locus of the movement.

Table 8

Societies Affiliated With the League of

French Language Societies

(Le Messager, 1961a, p. 10)

City of Lewiston
Institute Jacques Cartier
Ligue Du St. Nom (St. Peter)
Ass'n of St. Joseph
Ligue Du Sacre-Coeur (St. Mary's)
Ligue Du Sacre-Coeur (Ste. Croix)
Societe L'Assumption
Union St. Jean-Baptiste
Ass'n Canado-Americaine
Ass'n Des Vigilants
Club Jacques Cartier
Club Passetemps
Club Musical Litteraire
Club Sociale Le Montagnard
Union Locale Des Raquetteurs
Club Raquetteur Acme
Club Franco-Americaine
Club Des Travaillants
Ass'n Athletique Derby

City of Auburn
Ligue Du St. Nom
Forestiers Catholiques
Club Social

City of Brunswick
Societe L'Assomption
Union St. Jean Baptiste
Association Des Vigilants

City of Augusta
Societe L'Assomption
Association Canado-Americaine

Table 8 continued on next page.

31

City of Waterville
Societe L'Assomption

City of Westbrook
Ass'n De La Ste-Famille

City of Sanford
Societe L'Assomption
Union St. Jean Baptiste

Federation Canado-Americaine Du Maine

This fact alone seems sufficient evidence that there
was a close relationship between the movement and
the Church.

These affiliate organizations were relatively
autonomous and only loosely connected to the League of
French Language Societies. This autonomy is reflected
in the structure of organization of the League.

> "Each affiliated society keeps its
> statuses and autonomy and is not respon-
> sible for any debts contracted by the
> League of French Language Societies . . .
> The League deliberates and enacts within
> its constitution and its general interests,
> on questions submitted for study by the
> societies and their committees . . ."
> (Le Messager, 1961a)

The League was composed of two delegates from each
society. Again we find the flat, equalitarian form
of social organization so characteristic of the French.

The objectives of the League were rather vague:

> "To promote the Catholic, social and
> economic interests of French-Americans.
> To pave the way for sympathetic relations
> with different French-Language Societies
> in order to make our common efforts to
> protect Catholic and French interests in
> this country more effective . . . To
> work for the naturalization of our people
> and to study social and economic questions,
> in order to direct them (the French people)
> along the proper path and to teach them the
> obligations they must fulfill toward civil

and religious authority, America and their homes." (Le Messager, 1961a)

The generality of these objectives further illustrate the diffuseness of French social organization, and again we find the ideology to be phrased in moralistic and highly idealistic terms.

As we have mentioned, one principle of organization was redundancy and over-lapping membership. An example of this is the fact that the five officers (out of ten) from Lewiston of L'Union Americaine Des Raquetteurs represented four local organizations. These organizations were Le PasseTemps, Jacques Cartier, Le Montagnard, and L'Acme clubs. Further overlap is illustrated by the fact that Le Montagnard was a member of L'Union Americaine Des Raquetteurs, L'Union Locale Des Raquetteurs of Maine, Comite International Du Sport de la Raquette, and Le Ligue Des Societies de Langue Francais de Lewiston et Auburn (Le Messager, 1961a). Some of these societies were only local branches of national and international organizations in Canada and the United States, such as Le Montagnard, thus completing the interpenetration of organizations on a wider scale.

Further overlapping is seen between the French societies and the Democratic Party. This is demonstrated by the fact that out of 22 Presidents of French Culture Societies, eleven have been elected to public office (Le Messager, 1961b). Exactly which way the relationship operated is not clear. Perhaps all we can say at this point is that the politicians tended to be closely affiliated with the French Language Societies. Almost certainly they used these societies as a basis of political support, and the political machine in return provided leadership for the societies.

The size of these societies can be estimated roughly from known membership figures for several organizations. These figures were obtained from officers of the individual societies. Table 9 on the next page gives these membership figures.

Table 9

Membership in Selected French Language Societies in 1960

Cercle Canadien	800
Musical Litteraire Club	400
Le Montagnard Inc.	800
Pastime Club	400
Survivance Francaise	200

It should be noted that only three of these organizations were affiliated with the League of French Language Societies and that these represent some of the smaller groups. Given this, we may estimate the total membership in 1960 of French organizations. These organizations listed above have an average of 500 members. Since there were 28 French Language Societies, the total membership would be close to 14,000. There is no way, however, of estimating overlapping memberships so we really don't know how many people were involved. In any case this figure of 14,000 gives us some idea of the high degree of involvement in these societies. Just as a rough approximation let us assume that these 14,000 memberships represent 10,000 people (which is probably low). This means that almost half of the French adults belonged to some French Language Society, and in many cases, more than one. So we are dealing with a fairly extensive movement which reached a high proportion of the French community.

Also, some of the activities of these groups drew many non-members, which undoubtedly magnified their influence. For example, dances at the Jacques Cartier, Acme, and Pastime Clubs (which the investigator attended as a musician) drew crowds of 200 to 300 people, including many French youths who were too young to be members. Also such events as Snow Shoe Parades and St. Jean Baptiste festivals annually drew thousands of local townspeople.

In 1960, then, the French culture was virtually intact and showed signs of immense vitality as evidenced by organizational development, participation, political control, and even the emergence of a social movement. The events which were soon to follow could hardly have been predicted.

Chapter 3

Cataclysmic Culture Change

During the 1960's a cataclysmic shift in cultural
orientation became evident among the French-Americans
in Lewiston, with the French Culture being largely
abandoned, together with its supporting social struc-
tures. In its place came the mainstream, dominant,
American culture. The following analysis suggests that
gradual or generational cultural change is not always
the proper model for understanding culture breakdown
and eventual assimilation. Rather the data suggests
that some culture change may involve a "tipping-point"
when the whole culture and social system breaks down
suddenly, followed by a period of rapid assimilation.

Theorists building models of ethnic group breakdown and eventual assimilation generally visualize the
process as a series of steps progressing generation by
generation (Gordon). In other words, assimilation is
viewed as a generational process in which the younger
generation adopts to varying degrees aspects of the
receiving or dominant culture. The next generation is
assimilated to even a greater degree, and so forth.
Little has been written about other models of assimilation. The generational model has been widely adopted
in sociological circles as the primary if not the only
explanatory model.

A three generational model has been widely used
to describe this process. The first, or immigrant
generation, retains to a great extent its old ways,
participating in ethnic organizations, speaking the
ethnic language, and following the customs. The second
generation is often described as a marginal generation
caught between two cultures. On the one hand they are
subject to pressures from parents to retain their
ethnicity. From schools and other dominant institutions they are reinforced for becoming assimilated.
The third generation is usually fully assimilated and
rejects the ethnic culture. Often this generation
makes great efforts to disavow their ethnic heritage.
The fourth and succeeding generations sometimes come
back to an interest in their ethnic background,
exhibited interest in ethnic foods, holidays, history,
and knick-knacks. Nevertheless, their basic identity
is "American." In fact, it has been suggested that

35

only when one's new identity is secure does a person feel free to return to an interest in his or her ethnic heritage.

The French in Lewiston deviate markedly from this pattern. In the first place, the French had been in Lewiston for almost 150 years by 1960. The average French family had been there for four or five generations. By the second and third generation little assimilation had taken place. By the fourth and fifth generation, most still spoke French and participated in French institutions. Thus the three generational model is hardly adequate for describing this case. According to the three generational model we should have observed considerable assimilation by the second generation and almost full assimilation and acculturation by the third. By the fourth and fifth generations a fully assimilated French population should have been returning to a casual interest in French heritage.

A further deviation from the model occurred when assimilation in the fifth generation took a multi-generational form. Our generational model would have predicted that only the younger generation would become assimilated in this first step of the process. We found, however, from our study of language use that it was a multi-generational change. In other words, the French changed as a group. Our observations in both 1970 and 1973 revealed that there was little generational variability in the use of English in public places (e.g. stores, restaurants, banks, on the street). The only variability that was observed was in the over-sixty group and especially among women over sixty. Only this group appeared to use English less and French more than the general French population. In 1971 and 1973 several hundred conversations on the street were observed and only about 5-10 percent of all conversations were in French, whereas · as late as 1960, fifty percent of the conversations in the CBD were in French. This indicates that a generational model will not fit the French case in Lewiston. Only to a minor degree do generational differences enter the picture, and most likely explain only 10-20 percent of the variance in the use of French language.

A more exact model of the observed phenomena in Lewiston is suggested by Lieberson (1970) from his study of language change in Canada. He finds a sequence of French monolingual, followed by bilingualism,

and later English monolingualism. Using this model
with our data in Lewiston, what we find is essentially
the same sequence but with a different rhythm. The
first generation was monolingual French, the following
three generations were bilingual but speaking mostly
French, and by the fifth generation most were bilingual
but speaking mostly English. The shift then, in the
sixties, was a transition from a bilingual people from
a preponderance of French to a preponderance of
English-speaking. Seen in this way, the transition was
less radical than might appear on the surface. Nevertheless, the change was unusual, involving as it did
almost the entire French community.

It is the purpose of this paper to present an
in-depth case study of a culture which broke down
abruptly and whose members of every generation assimilated within a short time. This is not to say that
there were no signs of generational variability in
assimilation, but that they were relatively weak.

The explanation of this pattern, to be presented
more fully at the end of this paper, is that of limited
identity criteria. When group identity is based on
only a limited number of differentiating characteristics, loss of identity of the cultural group, and
consequent assimilation can be rapid or even
cataclysmic.

In this brief period of ten years, many changes
occurred which altogether served to indicate an abrupt
non-generational transition in cultural identity and
focus. In 1958 this investigator sampled conversations
in the central business district (Lisbon Street)
stores, including department stores, five and ten
stores, drug stores and restaurants. At this time
French conversations constituted roughly fifty percent
of the total. Later in 1970, when samplings were
repeated in the same manner, only ten percent of the
conversations were conducted in French.

Even as late as 1960 the French community in
Lewiston maintained a flourishing and cohesive culture.
Altogether there were 29 French Language Societies
with a total estimated membership of 14,000. Most of
these societies were bound together into a Preservation
of French Culture Movement. The Movement was directed
by The League of French Language Societies which had
as its aim "to spread and develop French culture in
this country." The League included also societies in

other Maine cities, but appeared to have its locus in Lewiston. Not only was a thriving social movement underway but also fifty-two percent of all Lewiston students were in French-speaking parochial schools (Assistant Superintendent of Schools), three out of four Catholic churches conducted their services in French (Church Office SS. Peter & Paul), and the French language newspaper had a wide circulation (Annual Review Edition).

Then came a cataclysmic cultural shift occurring as far as we can determine sometime between 1960 and 1970. In the 1970 sampling attention was paid to the possible generational differences in speaking French. There was little indication that speaking French was related to age of the subject, except among women over sixty.

In 1973, to confirm some of these findings an investigation was carried out, interviewing 20 businessmen on Main Street and upper Lisbon Street in Lewiston, which comprises the main business district. The businesses were selected to yield a sample of French as well as non-French establishments, and a sample of various types of business (e.g., large, small, financial, retail, service, etc.). The table on the next page lists the types of establishments contacted.

Lewiston, Maine

Table 10

Type of Establishments Contacted
in Businessmen's Survey by
Ethnicity

Type of Est.	French	Non-French
Financial		
Bank	1	
Service		
Restaurant		1
Shoe Repair	1	1
Travel Agency		1
Retail		
Clothing	2	1
Shoe	1	1
Jewelers	2	
Furniture	1	1
Hardware		1
Specialty	2	2
(camera, candy,		
gifts, books)		
Dept. Store		2
N=	10	10

*Note: The proportion of establishments which are French is fairly representative. This indicates that roughly 50 percent of all businesses are owned or operated by French people. This gives an indication of the degree to which the French have become established members of the business community.

Our procedure consisted of contacting the owner or manager who had been at the establishment at least since 1959. In some cases where managers were not available fitting this criteria, long term employees were interviewed. In most cases, however, the respondents were either owners or managers. The first question we asked was "what percentage of conversations in your store in 1960 were in French?" We received answers varying from 20 percent to eighty percent. The mean, however, was an even fifty percent. The median and modal response was also fifty percent, so we were dealing with a symmetrical, more or less normal distribution of responses. This finding fits exactly with the investigator's own estimates in 1958, as a result of observing conversations in stores and on streets in the CBD.

Since many non-French people from the city of
Auburn and outlying towns also shop here, the figure of
50 percent understates the prevalence of French speaking at that time among French people. Given that this
is a regional shopping center and assuming that roughly
30 percent of the shoppers are out-of-towners, (and
mainly non-French), the percent of French people in the
"shopping population" would be approximately 55 or 60
percent (deducting 15 percent for non-French Lewiston
residents). Thus our figure of 50 percent French
conversations is extremely high, given the fact that
only 55-60 percent of the shoppers were French. This
means that roughly five out of six French shoppers
were speaking French in public places in 1960. Granted
these figures are very rough, but we at least have
indicated the very high degree of French language use
in 1960.

The second question we asked the businessmen was
"What percentage of conversations in your store in 1970
were in French?" Obviously here we were trying to
measure any decline in the use of French language over
a period of ten years as perceived by businessmen. The
modal distribution of response being ten percent and
with over half of the respondents giving this answer.
Table 11 shows the distribution of both the 1960 and
1970 estimates.

Table 11

Businessmen's Estimates of French
Language Use in Their Stores, 1960 and 1970

Respondent #	1960 Est.	1970 Est.
1	10	5
2	20	10
3	35	10
4	35	10
5	35	35
6	40	10
7	45	10
8	50	10
9	50	10
10	50	10
11	50	10
12	50	20
13	50	50
14	50	50
15	65	20
16	70	35
17	70	70
18	75	30
19	75	35
20	80	10

The skewed distribution resulted in a mean of 22 percent. In order to access this unusual distribution we compared the responses of French vs. non-French businessmen, expecting to find the French businessmen giving higher estimates. We felt that they might be engaging in a bit of wishful thinking, perceiving more French conversations than actually occurred. We found, however, that French and non-French gave essentially the same mean estimate (22 and 23 percent respectively).

Another intervening variable that we felt might be affecting the responses was the location of the store.

We noticed that the stores at the south end of the area studied were closer to a lower class French ghetto, whereas the north end of the area adjoined areas populated by more English speaking people or upper status French, and was more accessible to out of town shoppers. We reasoned that shops closer to French areas would have more French shoppers and therefore the businessmen's estimates would be higher. We divided the stores evenly, 10 in the north and 10 in the south, and compared mean scores. Indeed, we did find a significant difference in the direction predicted. The north end gave a mean average of 15 percent and the south end 30 percent. Interestingly enough, the estimates for 1960 were not affected significantly by this ecological factor (the north end being 49 percent and the south end being 52 percent). This ecological factor, however, would not seriously affect the interpretation of the original average. If shoppers in the north end were different from the south end, we needed a sample of both to get an accurate over-all picture.

If we treat these numbers as estimates there is some reason to believe that the mean is not the most appropriate measure, given the skewness of the distribution. If eleven out of twenty have given 10 percent as their estimate, this would appear to constitute a considerable amount of agreement, especially given the random distribution of other estimates. Perhaps at this point a compromise figure between the mean and the mode, would be the most appropriate estimate. This would place our figure at 16 percent.

Other data collected at the same time (1973) throws some doubt even on this figure. Our interviewers were told to observe conversations on the street and in stores (both the north and south end).

41

Altogether, over an eight hour period one interviewer observed about 200 conversations. Although he did not write down each interaction, his estimate was that between 5 and 10 percent of the conversations were in French. In the stores he observed only one single French conversation. This, of course, was in January of 1973, not 1970. It may be that further attrition in the use of French occurred during that period, or that the businessmen's estimates for 1970 were inaccurate. It should be remembered that this investigator found only 10 percent French conversations in a survey of stores in 1970. So although there is some ambiguity about the exact amount of French speaking in 1970, the figure is probably between 10 and 16 percent. Assuming some attrition has taken place since then, which it probably has, only 5-10 percent of the conversations in 1973 in the CBD were in French.

The over-all picture, then, is one of dramatic decline in the use of French in Lewiston taking place during a ten year period. Whereas apparently 83 percent of French people were speaking French in public in 1960, only 25 percent were speaking French in 1970 (using the same computations applied in arriving at the 1960 figure). This means that roughly 58 percent of the French population discontinued the use of French in public places within a period of ten years. This figure alone would indicate that there was more than one generation involved in the discontinuation of French speaking. We found not only the teenagers speaking English in 1970 and 1973, but 30, 40, and 50 year-olds. We are dealing, then, not with a one-generational change, or even a two generational change, but a three generational change involving almost the entire French community. We will explore the reasons for this unusual pattern of assimilation in the following pages.

Further evidence of the decline in speaking French is a model cities survey (Ritter) conducted in model city neighborhoods in 1969-70. In this survey 83 percent of the respondents reported that their parents spoke French to them as a child. This is roughly equal to the total percentage of French people in Lewiston. Thus it appears that in almost one hundred percent of the cases French was spoken in the home among all prior generations. Only adults were interviewed thus reflecting the situation a generation or more ago. This is further evidence of the pervasiveness of French-speaking at that time. Substantiating this is data from the 1970 Census (U.S. Bureau of the

42

Census, 1970) which shows that 25,000 people in Lewiston listed French as their "mother tongue" in 1970. This represents 77 percent of the total French population.

Another indication of language breakdown was the cessation of the publication of Le Messager, the local French language newspaper in May 1968. In the mid-sixties it had dropped from a daily with a circulation of over 10,000 to a weekly publication with a circulation of only 2,200 in 1964 (Annual Review Edition).

Language breakdown even occurred in the parochial schools. In 1960 all parochial schools were either totally French speaking or bilingual, by 1972 they were all English (Assistant Superintendent of Schools). This is further evidence of the erosion of the French language during the 1960's and also probably one cause of the erosion. In 1960, 52 percent attended parochial schools, whereas in 1970 only 22 percent were parochial students.

By 1964 three of the four French parishes continued to conduct all French services, and only one introduced bilingual services. By 1972 all four churches had introduced bilingual services, although sixty percent of all services were still in French (Church Office). Obviously this indicates that the churches are lagging somewhat behing in the introduction of English. The reason for this probably lies in the fact that "the Church" has historically been the foremost supporter of the French Culture Movement and has always been the most ethnically conservative force in the community. One reason for this may be the preponderance of French clergy from Quebec who are more committed to French culture. Of the six priests at SS. Peter and Paul (the largest parish), all but one were French in 1971.

It appears that the existence of French masses may represent the one remaining vestige of French culture in an otherwise assimilated community.

These various indices all point to the mid-sixties as the focal point of a drastic breakdown in French language usage. This apparently occurred roughly between 1960 and 1970, a period of only ten years. The evidence also indicates that prior to this period French was widely used and encouraged. Nor does it appear that we are dealing here with a generational

43

change only. The evidence for this is found in several places. First the readership of French language newspaper was undoubtedly mainly adults, not the younger generation alone, yet it declined drastically to the point of extinction. Secondly, for adults to accede to English speaking parochial school system, their own will to retain the French language must have been weak. Thus again the breakdown cannot be attributed solely to the younger generation. Finally, we have shown that in 1971 the speaking of English in public places was distributed more or less evenly among all age groups, not just primarily among the under-twenties. Indications are, then, that this was more than just a generational change.

To further pinpoint this breakdown as being at about the mid-sixties, it was about this time (January 26, 1964) that the _Portland_ (Me.) _Sunday Telegram_ published an article on the breakdown of French culture in Maine (Fournier). The article contained an amazing admission of defeat by a "widely known Franco-American," who stated,

> "The new generation is losing overnight the essentials - language, culture and identity - which we fought all our lives to preserve. At this rate it won't be long before the great majority of our Franco-Americans will be such only in name, and nothing else."

It is instructive to notice that he views this as a very rapid ("overnight") change and that it is a generational change.

It is of additional interest, though, because it was (to my knowledge) the first public statement by a French community leader that all had been lost. In the same article (Fournier) another French community leader, Romeo T. Boisvert, pointed to the decline in readership of the local French newspaper and the increased mobility of the French community in answer to questions about "new directions" the French were taking. Also interesting is Fournier's comments after talking to a number of French leaders, when he says:

> "But most of these elder patriarchs now readily concede that like it or not, a new Franco-American way of life is inevitable."

This was, in a sense, a public "throwing in of the towel." Just three years previous it was the opinion of the French community that their culture would and must be preserved.

If language breakdown was the only indication of cataclysmic change, we would have a weak argument. However, fortunately, information was gathered which showed other elements of the French culture crumbling at about the same time.

Another indication of cultural breakdown was the clear increase in intermarriage during the sixties (see Table 12).

Table 12

Intermarriage Patterns in Lewiston, Maine, May and June 1960, and 1970 by Percent

Marriage Patterns	Year	
	1960	1970
French-French	50%	40%
French-non-French	24	38
Non-French-non-French	27	22
N =	(55)	(55)

The intermarriage data was secured by analyzing marriage announcements in the Lewiston Evening Journal for the months of May and June in 1960 and 1970. In 1960 the intermarriage rate (between French and non-French) was 24 percent of all marriages including Lewiston citizens and in 1970 the rate had risen dramatically to 38 percent. In 1970, French people were over-choosing non-French marriage partners. A purely random selection of partners would have resulted in only a 32 percent intermarriage rate, assuming that Lewiston alone was the relevant population. The fact that the adjoining city of Auburn borders on Lewiston and has only a thirty percent French population, makes it difficult to access the population base, and the resulting chance expectation of intermarriage. The 38 percent intermarriage rate, however, suggests that in all likelihood many non-French Auburn residents were being selected. Indeed we found that in 1960, 54% of the non-French partners were from out of town. In 1970

45

the figure had risen to 62%. In any case it is obvious
that the French population were showing an increasing
preference for non-French partners. It is also worth
noting that it was primarily French women who were
showing this preference. Out of the intermarriages in
the 1970 sample, approximately 3/4ths involved French
women but only 1/4th involved French men. In the 1960
sample a similar pattern was found.

Additional evidence is available concerning the
cultural breakdown in ethnic solidarity by examining
voting patterns. As we have observed earlier, most
councilmen and all city mayors since 1932 until 1970
were French (see Table 2). By 1970, although the
mayor was French, five out of seven councilmen were
non-French. Clearly a break had been made.

In 1971 and again in 1972, for the first time
since 1931, non-French mayors were elected. During
these years, four out of seven councilmen were non-
French (Mayor's Office).

Another indication of cultural breakdown occurred
within the most pivotal ethnic institution, the Roman
Catholic Church. Whereas fifty-two percent of Lewiston
students attended parochial schools in 1960, by 1972,
the number had dropped to 22 percent (Superintendent
of Schools). Reasons for this are varied, and partly
reflect a nation-wide trend, but include such things as
inadequate financing, closing of schools, and diffi-
culty in finding lay teachers. However, at least part
of the decline in enrollment was due to lack of interest on the part of the French population in ethnic
education for their children.

What happened to the French organizations during
this time is hinted at by Fournier's (1964) journalis-
tic researches where he concludes:
> "The French-Canadian societies which
> were dedicated to preserving the language,
> the customs, and the race's identity, are
> still in existence. But their role today
> is mostly devoted to socializing. Less
> than 25% of Maine's French-Canadians today
> belong to one of these societies."

An indication that the culture was disintegrating
at this time, is found in the rise in crime rates.
Table 13 indicates that certain categories of crime
rose much faster in Lewiston than in the rest of the
country during the late sixties.

Table 13

Comparison of Increase in Crime Rates in Lewiston
and the Entire Country, 1965-1970*
(Crimes Known to the Police)

	Crime Index	Murder and non-negligent manslaughter	Forcible Rape	Robbery	Aggravated Assault	Burglary	Larceny $50 and over	Auto Theft
Lewiston	+116%	-100%	+400%	+300%	+571%	+116%	+38%	+38%
U.S.	+ 90	+ 41	+ 62	+152	+ 55	+ 71	+87	+87
Excess in Lewiston	+ 26	-141	+338	+148	+516	+ 55	-49	-49

*Table computed from Uniform Crime Reports, Federal Bureau of Investigation,
1965-1970.

47

Aggravated assault rose (between 1965-1970) 571 percent, 516 percent more than the nation as a whole.
Robbery rose 148 percent more than the rest of the
country, burglary 55 percent more, and forcible rape
338 percent more. This investigator was assured by the
local Police Chief that there had been no significant
change in recording or reporting crimes during this
period. Assuming that the increase was real, it would
be difficult to prove that it was a result of cultural
breakdown but the rise in crime rates suggests that
there may have been a causal relationship between the
two variables.

It is interesting to note also, the kinds of crime
that were abnormally high in Lewiston during this
period. The two highest categories were forcible rape
and aggravated assault, both of which are crimes of
violence, rather than property crimes. The third highest category was robbery which involves the use or
threat of violence. Larceny and auto theft, however,
which are clearly property crimes showed a smaller increase than the national average. The only marked
deviation from this pattern is the drop in the murder
rate in Lewiston, but because there is less than one
murder per year there is no basis for computing a
meaningful percentage increase. This pattern of in-
creases in crimes of violence suggest that a great
deal of aggression and hostility was being expressed in
Lewiston at that time. Whether this aggression was
the result of culture breakdown and resultant frustra-
tion cannot be proven. However, this interpretation
is a reasonable one given the cultural climate among
the French at that time.

Under what conditions might we expect change to be
cataclysmic? Is there something about the culture itself which makes it susceptible to this kind of breakdown? One explanation which seems to fit this case is
that if the culture rests on essentially one differentiating factor and that factor is removed the whole
cultural identity is endangered. In this case the
differentiating factor was the French language.

French Canadians in Lewiston considered themselves
similar to the English (Yankees) except for their
language (and to some degree, religion). This was the
basis of their solidarity and identity as a group.
Religion would have served well also except for the
fact that there were many non-French Catholics also,
which would provide only a very rough distinction.

The surprising thing is that there were many "real" differences between Yankee and French culture, but the French did not see them. Yankee culture stressed stoicism, hard work, civic responsibility, puritanical ethics, and suppression of emotion. The "real" ongoing everyday culture of the French was different from their Yankee neighbors. Their "real" culture could best be described as humanistic.* So in reality the "real" cultures of French and "English" were considerably different. Had the French realized this, they would have had a solid basis for cultural identity and differentiation. But they persisted in seeing mainly their "ideal" culture" which happened to be very much like Yankee "real" culture.

So it appears that although real cultural differences might exist, a group must subjectively be aware of these differences if group cohesion and ethnic solidarity is to be maintained. Our theory, then, has to be amended to include this idea of subjectively perceived cultural differences as a basis of ethnic identity. Objective differences alone will apparently not do the trick.

To approach this in a slightly different way let us take the case of the American Jews. In their case the objective differences between Jews and Gentiles is not great culturally, especially among middle class, young populations. However, "subjectively" both Jews and Gentiles perceive that there are great differences between the two groups. The end result is that group identity is maintained but is based on more or less imagined cultural differences. We are reminded of W.I. Thomas' famous dictum, "Things defined as real are real in their consequences."

A further illustration of this principle as applied to social stratification is the relation of office workers to management. The average secretary apparently identifies with her supervisor even though there are wide differences in their life styles, values, and goals. She sees herself as being, in some sense, like him and identifies with him. As a result little class consciousness develops to drive a wedge between clerical workers and managers. Again, as in the French case, we find a lack of differentiation

*Note: The real culture of the French overlapped the Yankees in terms of hard work, and civic-mindedness.

resulting from the inability or unwillingness to perceive real cultural and social differences.

The French had never fully seen these differences and there is perhaps a reason why. The Catholic Church had for centuries educated their "flock" to think and feel in "ideal" Catholic cultural terms. In fact, it had discouraged and disparaged the "humanistic" elements in French cultural life. Lacking any other authority figures to present an alternative identity model, the average Frenchman adopted the Churches' version. Had there been a weaker church structure or a stronger alternative cultural identity model, the French might have recognized their most precious heritage; their humanistic culture which indeed made them different, made their culture rich and rewarding, and was the real basis of their solidarity for three centuries.

The triggering event precipitating cultural breakdown was language change. Why did the French language disappear so precipitously, in effect overnight? It is impossible to know all of the probable factors, but the following seem to be very important. First, it became non-functional to speak French when the French population became more upwardly mobile. In former years when most or many French people worked in the shoe factories and textile mills, speaking French was not a handicap. Then the mills left town (1950's) and they were forced to find other means of support usually involving some upward mobility and contact with English speaking people.

The high unemployment rate in the late fifties and all during the sixties resulting from the loss of industry, may have had a significant effect on cultural breakdown. The net result of this change in economic base was to change the occupational structure which we feel may have been a factor in initiating language change. Table 14 indicates a considerable shift in occupational structure from 1960 to 1970.

Table 14

Occupational Groups in Lewiston, Maine
1960 and 1970

Occupational Groups	Number Employed				% Change From 1960-1970
	1960	%	1970	%	
Prof., Tech., Kindred	1,270	8%	1,547	9%	+1
Mgrs. Off., & Prop.	1,201	7%	1,301	7%	---
Sales Workers	1,130	7%	1,045	6%	-1
Clerical and Kindred	1,625	10%	2,116	12%	+2
Craftsmen, Foremen & Kindred	2,078	12%	2,446	14%	+2
Service Except Pri. Household	1,311	8%	2,400	14%	+6
Operatives & Kindred	7,043	42%	5,723	33%	-9
Laborers Except Farm	698	4%	740	4%	---
Farm Laborers & Farm Foremen	42	.2%	49	.2%	---
Farms and Farm Mgrs.	36	.2%	32	.2%	---
Private Household Workers	233	1%	173	1%	---
Total	16,667	99%	17,554	100%	

Table 14 clearly indicates a significant movement away from factory work and an increase in service occupations. Also noticeable is a general upgrading of the labor force toward white collar and service occupations. These changes (which amount to about 10 percent of the labor force) channeled people out of factory work where English would be no asset, into occupations that required the use of English. Service occupations require dealing with "clients" who are English speaking, and clerical work requires the use of English to a high degree in day to day office routine. It must have become clear to some during this time that the old pattern of working in the mills was dying and that further opportunities would have to come from occupational mobility and eventual assimilation. Pushed out of their old patterns of work and therefore their life style, the only real alternative was to develop new occupational skills which in many cases involved learning English. This would be especially true if the French-speaking person hoped to enter the more rapidly expanding service industry where interaction with Yankees was inevitable. Thus an occupational dislocation may have been an important factor in encouraging occupational mobility and assimilation. The question of whether upward mobility aspirations were an important factor is pertinent at this point. Several questions posed by the Model Cities Survey (Ritter) are relevant to this problem. Keeping in mind that this was a working class sample (modal income was $66-80 per week) we find considerable satisfaction with their life style in 1969. Nearly two-thirds reported that they did not desire to move from their present house. Only twenty percent expressed interest in special high school night classes to obtain a high school diploma. Nor did many (twenty-eight percent) express interest in any kind of "special training." It appears that most people were not too unhappy about their status-position. Only thirteen percent thought their income was "a good deal below that what was needed." This indicates that whatever mobility aspirations existed were related to horizontal mobility and were due to pressure from the outside, such as the mill-closings, rather than from any dissatisfactions. Secondly, a new highway system (Maine Turnpike, 1950's) and television (1950's) came on the horizon in the mid-fifties which opened up the French population to enormous non-French influences. Previous to that, over one hundred years of living side by side with English-speaking people had probably eroded the ability and will to speak French since most people were bilingual by 1958.

The important thing, however, is that a flourishing culture became defunct over a period of 7-10 years and this was apparently a result of limited identity-criteria within this ethnic group. This single case, suggests then, that any cultural identity, no matter how well organized, is in peril if it is based on non-existent, limited, or unacknowledged differences.

The forgoing analysis has suggested several things which might have important implications for a theory of assimilation and acculturation.

First, we have suggested that it is possible for

52

assimilation to take place in a cataclysmic, sudden manner. In this community, cultural breakdown occurred in less than ten years. Not only was there a language breakdown, but also endogamy rules ceased to function effectively, and ethnic block voting virtually disappeared. Added to this was the fact that a flourishing social movement committed to maintaining and spreading French language and culture failed abruptly.

Secondly, we have suggested that the usual generational model of assimilation is not always the appropriate one for white American immigrants. We have shown that little assimilation and acculturation occurred for four or five generations, even though the three-generation model would have predicted assimilation by the third generation. When assimilation did arrive, it included virtually the entire community, not just the younger generation. It was a multi-generational change in which the community changed as a group.

Third, we have suggested that, contrary to the usual pattern, the French moved from their "real" culture which was very different from the Yankee culture toward their "ideal" culture which happened to be very similar to Yankee "real" culture. The usual pattern is for cultural identity to move ideal to real.

Finally, we have suggested that the underlying cause of cataclysmic cultural change is based upon limited differentiation from the environing culture or if the real differences are not recognized, decline and assimilation may be rapid, occurring in less than a generation. In the case of the French in Lewiston, the main perceived difference between the French and their host culture, as seen by the French, was language. When language broke down the culture collapsed. Empirically, many differences existed between the Yankee puritan culture and the French humanistic culture, but these differences were not readily recognized by the French, thus they could not provide a basis for ethnic identification.

Chapter 4

FINIS

Since the early seventies, we have continued to follow the course of French assimilation. We have found a continuation of the cultural and social assimilation outlined earlier. By now even the staunchest French activists believe that most of the French in Lewiston have become assimilated socially and culturally. The local newspaper articles have accelerated their admission of the radical loss of French culture. To document some of these later trends we have done some additional research.

First, we have visited the annual Franco-American Festival in Lewiston which takes place one week after 4th of July week in Kennedy Park in the middle of the old French millworkers section. Both in 1979 and 1980 we spent two hours at the festival. What we found was quite surprising. First, at neither time did we hear any French conversations, although we criss-crossed the area several times. The French we heard was not conversation but mainly Tin Pan Alley "French" songs belted out in a small circus tent. There was no group singing and indeed the wine served was from California not France. Also, there were only about 150 people there (even on Friday night).

In 1979 my brother-in-law (who is French) took me on a tour of lower Lisbon Street where he maintained we would most certainly hear some French. After one hour walking and one hour in a bar we heard none. The State Fair in Lewiston in 1981 again produced no evidence of French speaking.

We also repeated in the summer of '81 a survey of conversations in stores and streets, but this time the survey was extended to Auburn in the new shopping mall area, five minutes from Lewiston over a new bridge. Out of 50 observations in Lewiston (including two new malls which we had not studied before) there were no French conversations. Out of 50 observations in Auburn only one French conversation was heard between a middle-aged man and his wife. It seems clear that French on the street is dead. No accurate information could be obtained on French in the home but our restudy of Catholic Churches and schools indicated that French is declining in the bastion of French language (the

Catholic Church).

We found that no parochial schools used French, and one "French" school had closed.

Catholic French churches had also declined in the use of French. Of the four French churches, one had no French masses, and three averaged 65% French masses.

From several interviews I found that some French people still speak French in the home, but are usually underclass or working class people. This data is very shaky. In fact we do not know how many people speak French in the home, nor is there an easy way to find out. However, our data just presented on French schools and churches provide some indication that French is used some, in the most conservative indoor places (the churches).

A restudy of the political structure in Lewiston provides a mixed bag, during 1970-1981, three out of six mayors have been French which shows fewer French mayors than we would expect. On the other hand the composition of the City Council in 1981 was six French and two non-French, which shows less than expected but perhaps still some block voting. All in all it appears that ethnic politics are only minimally functioning.

I would like to mention an interesting interview with a woman and her daughter from the French elite. I cannot put too much credibility in our interview but this one is interesting because it raised some new issues. The older woman in the Summer of '81 gave me a one hour interview in her home. She spoke without an accent and seemed reluctant to give me answers to my questions. She vaguely suggested that the majority of French in Lewiston were Americanized culturally, and that French culture was all but dead, and that it was not fashionable to be French or speak French now. She also expressed hope that some of the French heritage could be retained. She seemed even to doubt that. Her daughter suddenly appeared on the scene interrupting the interview. The daughter was in her mid-30's and a Ph.D. She proceeded to say French culture was dead except for the lower class "bums" in the older French mill workers area. She became quite excited as she described these "bums" as lazy, sexually promiscuous, stupid, inclined to incest and the like.

More interesting perhaps was her description of what she called "Super-Americans" among the French. These, she said, were well educated, in their 30's or 40's or younger and had travelled widely. Super-Americans, she said, wanted nothing to do with French culture, disdained it and saw themselves as very much Americans. Again, if we can take her word for it, we find evidence of not only great cultural breakdown but even hostility toward French culture, and the negative label of being French developing among certain segments of the population. (which is often a third generation response in other cultures)

Of course, this was just one interview but it pointed to what might be a second turning point in the French community from being very French to French-Americans, to Americans and perhaps now to Super Americans.

To determine whether French was being spoken in secluded primary groups we had the choice of doing a telephone survey of families in Lewiston or observing French key clubs (bars).* We decided that a phone survey of families would yield biased results since French family members would not tell the truth to an anonymous interviewer (probably biased toward French speaking).

We finally decided to spend 1/2 hour in each of five French bars (afternoon of the 24th, December 1981). We intentionally chose bars (or key clubs) in the most heavily French, lower class area on Lower Lisbon Street where we would most likely hear French if any was being spoken. The results were quite surprising but in line with our expectations.

In three French key clubs no French was heard. In the other two key clubs only two French conversations were heard. One involved a 45 year old owner who reverted back to English and the second involved a bar-maid of about the same age who also quickly reverted back to English. In summary, out of a total of 53 conversations that afternoon we only heard two brief French conversations. Again, we should emphasize that these were places where French would be most likely to be heard.

So our recent data supports our earlier data and shows a distinct movement away from French culture.

*Note: which in many cases were vestiges of the old French language and culture associations.

Chapter 5

Implications for French Canada
And Ethnic Identity Theory

1. Implications for French Canada

What we have found in Lewiston, Maine may well shed some light on what is happening or may happen in the future in French Canada.

First, we have found the greatest vulnerability in French culture is the French language since it is viewed by French people as the main source of ethnic identity. To the extent that the French language is replaced by English, the French culture as a whole may well break down. The probability that the French language will continue to break down is increased by several factors in Canadian society. First, it is a <u>Mass Society</u> which means that mass institutions stemming mainly from English Canada through the mass media, mass organizations, mass politics, and mass production which will serve to force the use and exposure to English and English-Canadian culture. It would serve English interests well to encourage the penetration of English-based economic, political, media and other organizations into French Canada. This is already occurring.

The French in turn could best protect their language and culture by discovering and protecting the "real" sources of French ethnic identity; namely their unique "humanistic culture" which is vastly different from English culture. In a sense they must replace their "ideal" cultural identity with their "real" sources of identity which does not necessarily include the preservation of French language. The extent to which these conclusions are justified can only be tested by the future and perhaps very long term events in Canada itself.

2. Implications for Ethnic Identity Theory

Ethnic identity has long been thought to be a result of "real" ethnic differences. We have found that ethnic identity can be based on "false" or "ideal" views of ethnic differences. We have used the ethnic identity of American Jewish communities as an example of ethnic solidarity successfully sustained by largely "non-existent" differences with other ethnic groups. The French-Americans provide an example of a somewhat different process. They chose to see themselves in their "ideal" culture, similar to English culture leaving language as the only "real" source of identity to protect them as a group. In fact their real sources of differentiation and identity are varied and many (as many Frenchmen probably at some level know).

We have also found that a sudden collapse of ethnic identity may be a result of having too few sources of identity or not emphasizing real ethnic differences.

All in all, the more sources of ethnic identity (real or imagined) the better. Even imaginary sources of identity serve well.

Finally, we have perhaps stumbled on ways to undermine ethnic identity. The best way appears to be to somehow convince the ethnic "captive" group that they are really similar to host culture (even though this may not be the case). The second approach to undermine ethnicity is for the host "mainstream" culture to chip away at any central source of identity (through upward mobility, education, etc.) such as language among the French. Strategies to preserve ethnicity are just the reverse of the points just alluded to.

Conclusion

We have traced a group of French people over the course of four hundred years, analyzed their social structure, their culture, and its demise. Perhaps it would be useful at this point to summarize the high points of our analysis.

First we presented a short history of French immigration into Maine, and established that they are, in no sense, recent immigrants. They have, in many cases, been there for 150 years. We continued our analysis by showing the nature of French culture and social organization as it existed in Quebec and remained during the early days of in-migration.

A second section of the book showed the pattern of immigration into Lewiston (Maine) which indicates that the three generation model of assimilation, generally accepted by sociologists does not fit this situation. By 1960, the average French family had been in Lewiston four or five generations without a significant language breakdown and assimilation. According to the "three generation model," the third generation should have been virtually assimilated into the dominant "Yankee" culture. In this section we continued our analysis by examining the gradual evolution of French political power and organizational development. This analysis illustrated a number of characteristics of French culture and social organization that later proved useful in developing a model of social change. Our organizational analysis in the early 1960's also demonstrated the cohesion, strength, and integrity of French culture at that time.

During the mid-1960's a crucial event occurred which constitutes the focus of this book. About this time evidence of abrupt, even cataclysmic, breakdown of French culture and social structure occurred in Lewiston (Maine). We documented this in a number of ways, including language breakdown, organizational de-activation, changing ethnic voting patterns, parochial school decline, and a breakdown in endogamy rules.

We further, pin-pointed the breakdown as having occurred within a very short period of time, involving 7-10 years. An analysis of language patterns in the late sixties indicated that this was a multi-generational change and that the cultural breakdown affected all generations in the community, not just the young. This, of course, deviated from the usual pattern of assimilation and prompted us to see this as a cataclysmic and abrupt culture breakdown. The uniqueness of such a phenomenon demanded some kind of explanation.

Our prior analysis of French culture and social organization paid off at this point. We had found that he French had, essentially, two cultures. One was the "real" culture which we labelled as humanistic. The other was the "ideal" culture by which the French defined themselves, which we called puritanical. This constituted our theory of two cultures. The French often ignored real cultural differences between themselves and the "Yankees" and chose to define themselves in ideal terms which was very close to that of the environing "Yankee" culture. The main differentiating factor between the French (subjective) cultural identity and the surrounding Yankee culture was the French language. With such a limited basis for group identity, cultural decline was rapid when language differences were erased. This could be called the limited group identity theory of assimilation, when generalized beyond the present case to other groups.

Since language breakdown was the crucial "trigger" that caused this "cultural landslide," we examined the probable reasons that language breakdown had finally taken place after so many generations. The factors seemed to be, in retrospect, the gradual erosion of French language use over the years, a change in occupational distribution, the advent of American television, and an improved highway system.

It is with some nostalgia that we close this chapter on these French people, ending as they have, four hundred years of unique cultural adaptation under difficult conditions. It is all the more nostalgic given the usefulness and pleasure the old culture gave to its people. Whatever the reasons for its decline, we hope the best for them, as they enter the mainstream of American life.

References

Allen, James P.
1970 <u>Catholics in Maine: A Social Geography</u>,
unpublished Ph.D. Dissertation, Syracuse
University, 1970.

Annual Review Edition
1969 "French Language Newspaper Dies After 36
Years of Publication," in <u>The Lewiston Daily
Sun and Evening Journal</u>, (Lewiston Me.;
Feb. 4, 1969), p. 30a.

Assistant Superintendent
1972 The Assistant Superintendent of Schools in
Lewiston Maine, provided this information.

Church Office
1972 The Church Office of SS. Peter and Paul in
Lewiston provided this data.

Fournier, Norman
1964 "Franco-Americans Beginning New Era," in
<u>The Portland Sunday Telegram</u> (Portland,
Maine), Jan. 26, 1964.

Gordon, Milton M.
1964 <u>Assimilation in American Life</u> (New York:
Oxford University Press, 1964), The generational model is presented piecemeal on pages
71-78, 81, 107-108.

Guignard, Michael
1969 "The Franco-Americans: The Relationship
Between Ethnic Identification and Political
Behavior," Unpublished manuscript (Dept. of
Government, Bowdoin College), pp. 60-62.

H.A. Manning Co.
1970-71 <u>Lewiston City Directory</u>, 1970-71,
Vol. LXIII.

Hamon, E S.J.
1891 <u>Les Canadiens-Francais de la Nouvelle-
Angleterre</u>, (Quebec: Hardy, 1891); p. 17.

Hughes, Everett C.
1943 <u>French Canada in Transition</u>, (Chicago: Univ.
of Chicago Press, 1943).

Kennedy, Joseph
    1864 Population of the United States in 1860,
         (Wash. D.C.; Government Printing Office,
         1864), p. 200.

Knowlton, Evelyn H.
    1948 Pepperell's Progress: History of a Cotton
         Textile Company, 1844-1945, (Cambridge Mass.:
         Harvard University Press, 1948), pp. 166-167.

Lemaire, Herve B.
    1966 "Franco-American Efforts on Behalf of the
         French Language in New England," in Joshua
         Fishman (ed.), Language Loyalty in the
         United States, (The Hague: Mouton, 1966),
         p. 256.

Lieberson, Stanley
    1970 Language and Ethnic Relations in Canada.
         (New York: Wiley, 1970), see especially
         pages 25-30.

Maine Historical Society
    1972 "The Franco-Americans of Maine," by Gerard
         J. Brault, in Maine Historical Society
         Newsletter, Vol. 12, No. 1a (Summer, 1972).

Maine Sunday Telegram
    1972 "Franco-American Heritage Movement is
         Catching Fire," Maine Sunday Telegram
         (Portland, Maine), (March 19, 1972).

Mayor's Office
    1972 The Mayor's Office in Lewiston supplied
         this information.

Merrill, Georgia Drew
    1891 History of Androscoggin County, (Boston,
         W.A. Fergusson and Co., 1891).

Le Messager
    1961a Le Messager (French Language Newspaper pub-
           lished in Lewston, Maine) June 15, 1961.

    1961b Le Messager, Sept. 14, 1961.

Michaud, Charlotte
    1971a "Recognizing Maine's Ethnic Groups," in
           The Maine History News, (Lewiston, Maine,
           July, 1971), pp. 4-5.

1971b "Franco-Americans in Maine," in The Maine
          History News, (Lewiston, Maine, October,
          1971), pp. 4 and 8.

Miner, Horace
     1939 St. Denis, A French-Canadian Parish,
          (Chicago: University of Chicago Press, 1939).

Parsons, Talcott
     1951 The Social System, (Glencoe Ill: The Free
          Press, 1951), pp. 46-51, 58-67.

Paroisse Saint-Pierre et Saint-Paul
     1971 Centenaire Album Souvenir (Lewiston, Maine,
          1971).

Reilly, Wayne E.
     1971 "Little Canada: Maine's French-Canadian
          Heritage, in Trouble on an Urban Island,"
          in The Maine Times (Topsham Maine), Vol. 3,
          No. 49, (Sept. 10, 1971), pp. 12-15.

Ritter, W. Stuart
     1970 The Lewiston Model Neighborhood Area:
          A Comprehensive Community Planning Survey,
          (Lewiston Maine: Lewiston Model City
          Committee, 1970).

U.S. Census Office
     1901 Twelfth Census of the United States: 1900,
          Vol. 1, Population, Part 1 (Washington, D.C.:
          Government Printing Office, 1901), p. 189.

U.S. Bureau of the Census
     1931 Fifteenth Census of the United States: 1930,
          Vol. 1, Population, (Washington, D.C.:
          Government Printing Office, 1931), p. 474.

     1961 U.S. Census of Population: 1960, Vol. 1,
          Characteristics of the Population, Part A,
          Number of Inhabitants, (Washington, D.C.:
          Government Printing Office, 1961), pp. 21-22.

     1963 U.S. Census of Population: 1960, "General
          Social and Economic Characteristics: Maine,"
          (Washington, D.C.: Government Printing
          Office, 1963).

1972 U.S. Census of Population: 1970, "General
Social and Economic Characteristics: Maine,"
(Washington, D.C.: Government Printing
Office, 1972), Table 102.

U.S. Department of the Interior
1883 Statistics of the Population of the United
States at the Tenth Census: 1880, Vol. 1,
Population, (Washington, D.C.: Government
Printing Office, 1883), p. 199.

Vicero, Ralph D.
1968 Immigration of French Canadians to New
England, 1840-1900: A Geographic Analysis,
unpublished Ph.D. Dissertation, (University
of Wisconsin, 1968).

Bibliography

Association Canado-Americaine
52 Concord St.
Manchester, N.H.   03100

Project F.A.R.I.N.E. (Franco-American Resources
      Inventory of New England) working from FAROG
      Office, list scheduled to be ready in fall of 1979

      FAROG Office
      Fernald Hall
      UMO, Orono, ME   04469   (207) 581-7082

Mallett Library, for information, write to:
      Librarian
      The Mallett Library
      Union Saint-Jean-Baptiste
      1 Social Street
      Woonsocket, R.I.   02895

National Materials Development Center (NMDC) for French
      168 South River Road
      Bedford NH   03102

            for information on projects in progress, for
            ideas, as center for possible publication on
            local materials

A Resource Guide for New England Libraries, Hagel,
      Phyllis, NADC, Wellesley College, Cambridge, MA

      Maine State Library
      Augusta Maine   04330
      toll free phone: (800) 452-8793

            A selective list of review, selection, and
            cataloging aids for use with Franco-American
            materials, annotated, with sources, by topic.

ABOUT THE AUTHOR

Dr. James Hill Parker is
currently Professor and Chairman
of the Anthropology and Sociology
Departments at Long Island University, Brooklyn Center. A native of
Auburn, Maine, he received his Ph.D.
in Sociology from the University of
Iowa in 1965. He is the author of
32 professional articles, including
articles in Social Forces, Sociology
and Social Research, Human Organization, and the New York Times. He
has just completed two other books:
one, Social Games in Conversations
and Small Groups, and a second on
Organizational Games. He has also
recently published a book titled,
Principles of Urban Sociology.
(University Press of America, 1982).